Made in the USA
Las Vegas, NV
10 May 2024

89770707R00115